HONOR ONE ANOTHER

The ABCs of Embracing Our Spirit Within

HONOR
ONE ANOTHER

The ABCs of Embracing Our Spirit Within

Virginia Alice Crawford

PUBLISHED BY

HONEYSUCKLE PUBLISHING, LLC

San Antonio, Texas

PO BOX 1163   THREE RIVERS, TEXAS 78071

Published in 2020 by
Honeysuckle Publishing, LLC
San Antonio, TX

Cover design by Tabitha Crile.

ISBN 978-1-7346934-0-9
Library of Congress Control Number: 2020914911

Printed in the United States of America.

This book is written in loving memory of
my daddy, Charles L. Cameron, Sr.,
whose spirit lives forever in my heart.

Preface

Dearest Reader,

I can recall as a very young child, lying on my back in the dark and smelling the freshly cut grass my dad had mowed earlier in the day. I would stare up at the endless twinkling stars and be in awe. I questioned who I was and why I was alive. This book, Honor One Another: The ABCs of Embracing Our Spirit Within, is a result of all those many years of soul-searching, that personal search for my connection between being born into existence and my specific purpose for being in this world.

It could be that you too have done this very same thing. Like me, you may have questioned if you have a spirit. You may have searched for a clearer understanding of yourself. You may have wondered if you are fulfilling your best self. You may still be questioning your place in this world. Like you, I have been there, at different times in my life. I have wanted a better connection to my authentic self, and yet, I didn't know how to find it. And, I have—for as long as I can remember— searched for who I am.

Today, I am closer to the me that I believe I am meant to be. And, I believe, everyone who seeks a better connection to themselves will—in time—find what they are searching for. Whatever you are looking for, it is my hopes that you will find a little bit of help in the pages of this book. This is not a how-to book, nor will it provide all the answers you may be searching for. But, perhaps, something I am sharing with you, and have written here, will inspire you to figure out what step to take next in embracing your spirit more fully.

It is important to know that we each connect with our spirit much better at different times in our life than when someone else might. We are all different. We are meant to find our way at our own pace. Therefore, we need different people in our lives at different times from parents and grandparents to school friends and teachers to professors and mentors to employers and co-workers and even to writers and artists—all who help us to find our purpose in this life.

Sometimes, I think—rather than finding our purpose—it finds us. We just don't know how to embrace it. I also believe we don't realize how closely our purpose is tied to how we acknowledge and accept our spiritual self. It is my hopes, as you read this book, that you will come across an idea that will bring you more fully into who you are—this spirit with a personality like no other. Sure, we can resemble our mother or father or some of our siblings or take on habits of friends or co-workers, but ultimately, we are made up of DNA, traits, characteristics—and likes and dislikes—all our very own.

In pondering how to share my ideas and experiences with you, I decided that perhaps a fun book would be nice. Something easy to read, all at once, or one day at a time, until finished. Instead of writing a book with 365-pages, one for each day of the year, or even 52 pages for 52 weeks, I felt 26 short chapters or pages would be more than enough to accomplish this, and get you excited about embracing your own spirit more fully. And what better way than an "ABC" book. Being a grandmother today certainly is having its influence on me.

Whether you eventually found what you were looking for, or perhaps are still searching, may this book inspire you to embrace your spirit in a way that will bring you to the centeredness of the life you are seeking. Perhaps, like me, you will become closer to discovering your purpose—and not only embracing but also accepting your spirit—in a much needed and more meaningful way.

With love,

Virg

Foreword

Dear Reader,

When my good friend, Virg Crawford, asked me if I would write a few words for this book—Honor One Another: The ABCs of Embracing Our Spirit Within—I was thrilled and flattered. Virg and I met about 25 years ago in Kingwood, Texas where we were teamed up for a year as ninth grade religious education teachers at our local church. After that year ended, Virg went on to teach fourth grade for a few years, and we met up again when we studied together in a Formation Toward Christian Ministry course. More recently, I have had the distinct pleasure of working with her in her capacity as secretary for St. Brigid Parish in San Antonio, Texas. It was during some of my visits to the parish office that Virg confided how much she loves writing.

I was attracted by the gentle and meaningful way she wrote about the spirit within each of us. And the simplicity of using the Alphabet to express the attributes of our spiritual selves was unique.

You'll find this book, with its short chapters, to be an easy read. You can either devour it in one sitting or savor it for days, reading one chapter a day or even one chapter a week. Personally, I preferred reading one or two chapters a day as a source of wisdom and inspiration during my morning meditation and prayer.

But don't let its brevity fool you. It's packed with little nuggets of gold that reveal 26 ways to embrace your spirit so you can attain love, peace, faith, inspiration, and other aspects of human experience that we all deserve. Any of the messages will speak to your heart.

Take Virg's thoughts on Kindness, for example. If we are to become loving spirits, we must show kindness to others. While others can certainly hurt us when they are neglectful—the thank you note that never came or the missed appointment—be aware that we, too, can act the same way toward others. Kindness, therefore, calls us to take time for others, to be considerate and, most of all, to be loving.

Just like the ABCs of any topic provide us with the basics of that topic, this book is like the ABCs of spiritual growth. It is a primer on how we can be our best and give our best. Putting its tenets into practice can make our lives happier and healthier. And whether we read the first chapter, the last chapter, or any chapter in between, we'll feel the love and inspiration that are there for us.

From my perspective, Virg writes like your best friend . . . someone who celebrates your successes and consoles you when you are down. And like a true friend, this book will bring out the best in you.

Read it. Meditate on it. Then apply her alphabet of spiritual literacy to enhance the spirit within you.

With all best wishes,

Joseph Lilli

Bio: *Joseph Lilli has spent more than four decades as a writer, author and communicator. His career includes writing for television and radio news, a daily newspaper, a major independent advertising agency, and a major independent public relations agency. Currently a freelance writer, he writes articles for several magazines and creates marketing communications for corporations. He has also authored four books for clients.*

Special Appreciation

I would like to thank everyone who has ever encouraged me to publish my writings or to become a published author. Your words of encouragement and support have not gone wasted. I have finally heard you, and this book is just the beginning. Thank you.

I want to especially thank my mom, Majina Palomin Cameron Foster, for always supporting me in my writing through the years. I appreciate you, Momma Love, for always being my cheerleader. I am still so honored for your hiring me all those years ago to create your baking business brochures and allowing me to include suitable writings. More recently, thank you for showing no surprise when I told you that I had finally written a book which was almost ready to go to press. Your warm, loving, and accepting reaction is a treasured memory.

I thank my loving husband, Charles Wade Crawford, for his undying patience, especially in our early years as I labored late into the nights doing cut-and-paste for several family newsletters (before we owned a computer), finishing writing class assignments, and polishing articles for community newsletters. As I wrote this book, Charles, your sweet words of support have touched me more than you will ever know. The little tweaks you offered here and there are very much appreciated.

Thank you to my siblings, Charlie, Vicky, Veronica, John, Vanessa, Violet and Verna, for your love, and for giving me plenty to write about—in future books. Your antics growing up will make great reference points (wink, wink).

Thank you to my teachers, from grade school through college, for taking time to encourage me to develop my knack for research and creative writing, most especially, Joy Welch (3rd) and JoAnne Doffing (12th). Thank you also to my recent online writing course instructor, Eva Shaw, for seeing the writer in me.

To my dearest of friends: Iris, Melissa, Tricia, Pam, Terrie, Fabiola, Carol, Nancy, Jessica, and Heidi-Rose and all those whom I cannot name here as, frankly, there are many, thank you for touching my life so very deeply and uniquely. Your love and acceptance of me over the years mean more to me than silver or gold. (Rest in peace, my dearly missed friends, Grace R. and Carmen I. *Te amo*.)

Thank you to my brothers- and sisters-in-law for your constant love and friendship over the years and for participating in my early family newsletters.

A special thank you to Tabitha Crile, my niece and my artist, for such a lovely book cover. Your amazing skill and creativity, Tab, captured my vision of the design I was looking for. Thank you so very much.

Thank you to Joseph Lilli for saying Yes to writing this book's Foreword. Your kind words, Joe, have given my book a new dimension. I am profoundly grateful to you for that and for all the time you have devoted to this project.

Thank you to my "readers," Veronica Cameron, Tabitha Crile, Vi Daniels, Joe Lilli, Iris Solcher, Grace Torline and Nancy Witte, who all spent time reading and editing this book for publication. Having your extra sets of eyes has made all the difference. Your recommendations were more than welcome and very gladly received. Each correction and suggestion have made this book much better than it was at the start. Thank you from the bottom of my heart.

A special shout-out to "Vee" for ultimately giving me the encouragement to write this book. Plus, I knew that if I didn't write for publication, you would never stop bugging me about it. Thanks for being such a pest!

Thank you to my friend and spiritual director, Priscilla Salinas, who not only encouraged me to take up journaling again but also believed I would one day write and publish many books. Priscilla, your faith in God's timing has been spot on.

And, finally, thank you to James Scott Bell for writing a book (How to Make a Living as a Writer; 2014) that inspired and motivated me to make it through the writing and publishing process. Well done.

Introduction

We are all born with a spirit, that part of each of us that makes us who we are. This spirit of ours lives in our body along with our mind and our heart. This is what makes us, as human beings, so unique. It is our essence. And I am sure, like me, you have wondered if our spirits continue to live on even after life on this earth has ended. This questioning is an important part of our journey. But I also believe it is just as important for us to first admit that we have a spirit.

Now, I realize most everyone has their own idea about whether we have a spirit and how to nurture it, and if we should spend our time in nature or worship God in a formal setting. I know many people who are of different faiths and a few others who are not sure that they believe in God or a higher power. I do my best to respect everyone's feelings, but I also feel strongly that each of us are made up of more than a body. We each have a spirit that makes us who we are, that gives us our unique personalities. And, I believe to acknowledge that each of us is a spirit, on the same journey, is a good start.

On this earth, to be a living, breathing being, we must have a spirit. I have learned to deny this fact can lead one down a winding path of soul-searching, along with feelings such as despair, loneliness and depression. The sooner we embrace the idea that we have a spirit, that we are a spiritual being, the sooner we can find our true selves and the unique purpose we were created for. By embracing this concept, we can achieve a better way of living—spiritually.

Through spirit, we can be in awe of our universe and this planet...our living, breathing home with its change of seasons and fuel-providing abilities. We can accept and appreciate our miraculous body with its five senses and capacity for movement, fitness and healing. And we can be amazed by our spirit, with mind, heart and soul working in tandem to give each of us the most unique of personalities. Loveable. Human. Growing. Learning. Inspiring. Fascinating. Surely, acknowledging that we are spirits in bodies, or bodies with spirits, can only move us toward embracing ourselves more fully.

To suggest that we do not have a spirit can give the idea that everyone is the same. However, when I look into anyone's eyes, hear them speak, watch them interact, I can only see how unique we each are. From the time I can remember being able to think and to reason, I felt not only was I special but so was everyone else around me. It was interesting to see my parents interact with their families and how my siblings, much to my angst, seemed to have a mind of their own. I could see that we were each very individualistic, with feelings and thoughts all distinctly our own. I wondered if they could see this too or just took for granted what and how life was, without questioning anything. It could be that I had way too much time on my hands, or that I was simply born with an inquisitive spirit.

This inquisitiveness has played out constantly in my life. I was born the eldest daughter of eight children. My dad was Presbyterian growing up and converted to Baptist in his first marriage. My mom grew up Catholic. Neither one was practicing. My mom used to read to us about Jesus. She would tell us how some people believe he is the Son of God while others believe he was only a very good person. She told us when we grew up that we could choose for ourselves what to believe.

When I was 13 years old, and while I was staying several hours away with a cousin for a few months, my family started going to a local non-denominational church. I eventually got baptized, but I left that faith in my early twenties. I found that as I searched for my fuller identity and purpose in life that I wasn't satisfied with the answers to the questions I was seeking. I believed in God and had done so since my early years as a child, reinforced each time I viewed the stars and vast universe from my front yard. However, I believed there had to be another way of honoring Him living in me.

Today, I am Catholic and one of the things I love about this Faith is the freedom it gives me to practice my spirituality. Since I struggled for so many years searching for the best way to communicate with my Creator, I feel truly blessed to have found this Faith and be at this place in my life. It is a Faith where I can worship

God and be free to pray and meditate in many forms. It allows me to embrace my spirit more fully, as I continue to grow toward being a better person every day.

So, what makes me qualified to write about honoring and embracing our spirit within? Mostly, the school of hard knocks and everything that makes me who I am, most especially my desire to inspire others through my writings. I have learned a lot about the human spirit from my experiences in childhood, school and work; living in different places; the friends who I have chosen or who chose me; and my unique personality and basic life philosophy. My hope is that I can share some of these insights with you, and that you can glean some little diamond in the rough to make your life and spirit all the better from reading it.

When planning this book, and how I would share all I have learned in my life about embracing my spirit, I considered titling it, Kaleidoscope. Have you ever looked through a kaleidoscope? I have looked through many and they have always amazed me. Even as a young child, their simple yet complex beauty made me think about how multi-faceted we are as living beings. All the colors gleam so beautifully and change constantly at every small turn of the dial. Our beings do the same thing. With every new day, every new encounter, every new thought, we ourselves change, too. We can become more beautiful inside, happier, content…or we can become tired, sad, even angry. With every moment, we are evolving, learning, and discovering. And, with every change, we can neglect or nurture our spirit.

Another title for this book that I considered was Namaste, which means "I bow to the spirit within you." If only we were all raised with the belief or idea that it is a high honor to treat each other with reverence. Somehow, when we first see another person, we see them as bodies rather than spirits. Seeing people only as bodies, or as bodies first, can cause issues. As humans, we tend to judge what we see. We base whether we like someone on their looks; how they are dressed; the color of their eyes, hair or skin. We envy others for their nice clothes or neat features. We get jealous of others. Looking different makes people nervous. But what if we first seek to see each other as spiritual beings?

It is said that the eyes are the windows to the soul. Perhaps, the next time we meet someone or speak with a friend or family member, we could take time to look into their eyes and really see who they are—not how they look, but what they are saying, thinking, feeling. We might be surprised at what we find. Ultimately, we will come to see people as spirits rather than clothes-clad bodies. As our own spirit evolves, we will see others for who they are, not what they present to us as we look at them. We will see in their eyes: happiness or sadness. We will hear in their voice: grief or joy. We will respond gently in honor to each spirit we meet—whether friend or stranger. This is definitely an amazing thing.

Well, it's almost time—time to start reading. You can read this book from front to back, back to front (as I am guilty of doing), from center out, one "letter" per day or all in one day. No matter how you choose to read it, I encourage you to keep a journal with you to make notes about your own discoveries. If you dare, perhaps, you might prefer to write on the pages of the book itself. I have seen many books over the years with notes written on the inside or outside margins or at the top or bottom, and I always think how wonderful that someone loved the book so much as to add to it their own notes, thoughts and musings.

It is my hope that as you read this book's pages that even just one thought will inspire you to embrace your spirit more fully and to bring you closer to a more beautiful you. If it does, then taking the time to put my thoughts into words, and making this book happen, will have been worth it.

Happy reading!

"Unlike a drop of water which loses its identity when it joins the ocean, man does not lose his being in the society in which he lives. Man's life is independent. He is born not for the development of the society alone, but for the development of his self."

~B. R. Ambedkar

Contents

HONOR ONE ANOTHER

The ABCs of Embracing Our Spirit Within

A is for Ageless

"eternal"

Most people seem to feel younger than they really are. Our bodies age and we track every year by celebrating our birthdays. We live our lives as though we will live forever. There are those people who participate in daring sports, and those who neglect their bodies or put things in it not meant to be. But, our spirit—who we are inside our heart and mind—is eternal and never seems to age. Our spirit stays as young as our outlook on life. A person can often go for years feeling like they are still 20 or 30 or 50, even though their muscles are not as taut as they used to be, or take longer to recover when exerted, and their skin wrinkles or sags depending on the care that it has been given. But, as our body ages, our spirit simply becomes more ageless.

Our spirit is meant to last beyond this life on earth into the life ever after. When we embrace the idea, or fact, that our body will die and that our spirit will continue to live on, we can then see ourselves with a truer perspective. We can realize that our focus should be on developing our spirit—who we are—along with keeping our body healthy for as long as it will last on this earth, so that we are the best versions of our spiritual selves when we pass from this life.

Are you caring for your body and spirit so you can live a longer life or merely living day-to-day as if there is no tomorrow? Are you caring for your body and spirit by getting enough rest, nutrition and fitness, and loving interaction with others, so that you can continue to be your best "you"? Are you challenging yourself, or spirit, to grow in positive ways?

Take some time today to consider what ageless means to you.

B is for Beatitude

"perfect happiness"

A Beatitude is a proverb-like blessing. It comes from the Latin word *beatus*, meaning both "happy" and "blessed." The word Beatitude is usually attributed to being kind, humble, merciful, compassionate and peace-making.

By practicing Beatitudes, we can achieve a state of happiness that stress, anxiety or depression cannot touch or take away. As human beings, we regularly search for happiness. We do this in many ways. Sometimes these ways bring us happiness and other times not. By understanding what we want from life, what our purpose is, where we hope to be in 10 or 20 years, we can find true happiness.

However, as we search for happiness, we can become stressed, depressed, lonely, and even sad. This is because we focus on becoming happier instead of enjoying what we're already blessed with. When this happens, we can ask ourselves what we can do to refocus our life or spirit. How can we become happier yet not be caught up in the pursuit of happiness?

It could be by focusing on the present and reaching out to others, especially those in need. Growing up, I admired people who could put others at ease during difficult times, particularly illness or death. I questioned what these individuals had which made them so caring and giving. I soon realized that they could identify and put another's spiritual and physical needs before their own. Once I started to practice this action, I started to become a more caring spirit as well.

Today, I am more of that Beatitude of compassion that I still admire in others. What are some Beatitudes you would like to achieve or own? Try to think of one Beatitude today that you can grow in. What is it? Do you know?

C is for Community

"a place of connection"

Spiritual beings need community with others as much as they need quiet, reflective time. No matter how shy or reclusive a person is, everyone needs connection to others. As spiritual beings, we seek positive acceptance from others. This builds a stronger sense of self, giving us that emotional strength that we need to eventually fulfill our higher and individual purpose. When we don't get that sense of community, or instead receive negative feedback, we shut down or act out in ways that are not becoming or fulfilling of our higher purpose.

To be our best selves spiritually, a healthy balance of quiet time alone as well as a good relationship to others can be the solution. If we don't get the positive connections we need, and therefore choose ones that instead harm us, our spirit reflects this, and we suffer rather than benefit.

Think about your community, the fellow spirits or friends that you share your life with, those that help fuel your days. Are they bringing you the things you are seeking? Peace. Contentment. Higher learning. Or, are they instead bringing drama, discord, or separation to your life?

Good connections are important to a healthy spirit. Walking away from those who are not feeding your soul in the ways you need might be what your spirit needs of you to be the best "you." Community should be nurturing in every way that counts to you. Is it? Are your connections nurturing you? Take time today to consider how you can improve your connection to others in a positive and uplifting way. It might be just as easy as sending a greeting card by mail or through email, or a quick text or phone call. Come on, you can do it.

D is for Dancing

"rhythmic movement"

Close your eyes. What do you see? What do you feel? As spiritual beings, we seek rhythm in our lives. Even the disorganized person searches for some sort of order, or routine of comfort, that brings accomplishment and peace in their otherwise chaotic day. When we stop or slow down long enough to listen to our spirit, we learn what we need to achieve our goals, our dreams, our inner longings. Whether we listen to our favorite music or to our inner voice, moving rhythmically—either slowly or quickly, can bring us to new discoveries of self and to a new understanding of our spirit in relation to our whole self—and to others.

If you have ever wondered if dancing is that good for you, just ask my pup, Sammie. She loves to dance. The moment I turn on music or she sees me and my husband dancing, she wants up in my arms so she can dance, too. It is so cute. I have never seen an animal or pet love to dance like she does. This got me to thinking. How important is dancing to our spirit? And why do some people seem naturally inclined to be good dancers and others not—as though they really do have two left feet? Perhaps it is about letting go, feeling free to enjoy the beat of the music and trusting we won't look like total idiots if we get up and "move it" just a little bit. How about you? What is your spirit telling you when you listen to your favorite song? Why not just dance to it and enjoy? It could be the beginning of a new relationship with your spirit, certainly a new aspect of it.

So, put on your dance shoes and get to tapping those toes. Enjoy some rhythmic movement and let your spirit soar to new heights or be filled with calm. Let dance help you be more fully connected to the you that you want to be.

E is for Everyday

"usual routine"

Spirituality is a part of our everyday life. It took me a while to learn this.

Because I didn't know who I was or what my purpose was, I would go days, weeks, even months without questioning what my inner being needed. Since I like to be structured and organized, I would do everything that I "needed" to do, without slowing down to acknowledge the whole being that I am. I would get up, go to work, get off work, do chores, and then do it all over again without slowing down for much else. But then, I learned if we are spiritual beings, it should be our usual routine to nurture our spiritual selves, just as we do our physical bodies.

Maybe because we cannot see it, we tend to neglect our spirit. I know I used to. Once I realized that my spirit needs as much attention as my body does, I began to listen to it. Not just once a month or once a week, but every day. I started to take time to read, go for long walks, enjoy bubble baths, sneak in a movie on an unexpected free afternoon...or use the time to meditate. That's right, just be. I found out that taking time to reflect, to spend more time in nature, and to learn to be alone with myself are all great for the soul.

Soon, I saw a difference. Instead of being too listless or without direction, I became energetic, eager to meet my day. All because I slowed down long enough to listen to my spirit—every day—not just occasionally or hardly ever.

Our spirit lives in us every single day, for as long we are alive on this earth, and will be with us for eternity. It only makes sense that we should listen to it—routinely. How about you? Are you listening to your spirit? What is it telling you about your everyday routine?

F is for Faith

"complete trust"

Often, our spirituality is affected by our ability or inability to trust others, sometimes even to trust our own self. If we learn to completely trust ourselves, we can have better relationships, success in our careers, and connections to what is important to us.

To have complete trust in ourselves, we must embrace our spirit in the most basic way—unconditionally. For some of us, this is easy. We can trust that our higher power is watching out for us and leading us to our best self. But, for some, it is difficult. We find it hard to let go and completely trust that all will be well in our life and world. It could be that our trust was once betrayed, or that we haven't taken opportunities to show that we are trustworthy. Once we learn to trust our spirit just a little, by listening and looking for the opportunities available to us, we slowly become more trusting. Eventually, we learn to fully trust our spirit to lead us in positive ways, and the beauty we experience from this only grows.

Can you trust your spirit to know what is best for you? Do you know yourself, or spirit, well enough that you can completely trust it, or God or your higher power, to help you make the best decisions for yourself? Faith helps us know that we are heading in the right direction. Start today and embrace your spirit with faith, so that you are on the right path, or soon will be. Do you feel that you are? What can you do to have more faith in your life? If you listen closely, you might be surprised by what your spirit is telling you. So, listen more intently. Let your spirit help you by being ready to completely trust it to know what you need—not just today, but every day.

G is for Grit

"determination"

It does a spirit good to have a fair amount of grit or determination. This gives us what we need to stay the course. Often, in life, we are not told that going to college, getting and keeping a job, or staying married will be the challenges they end up being. So, when the going gets tough, some of us can give up too soon. Our spirits are then not only forced to deal with disappointment but also the challenge of finding a new job, choosing a different career, or learning to live alone. If we know who we are, and we trust our spirit to be led by that higher power or supreme being, then having grit will help us to work through the tough times.

There have been times for me, as I am sure there may have been for you, when life has gotten a little tougher. In hindsight, some of these times may have been easier than others. Like sticking to a job when it was not the right fit until a more suitable job could be found. Or when we learned of major news affecting our health or living circumstances, or when a loved one passed away. Grit helps us to get through these times, so that our spirit does not succumb under their weight.

Also, being determined to reach our goals or seek our unique purpose can benefit our spirits positively. Does your spirit have grit? Can you hold fast in the tough times of your life? What can you do to get more grit or determination in your life and not give up? Do you know someone you can talk to who has true grit? What do they do to succeed past the obstacles in their life?

When our spirits have grit, we can tackle the most mountainous tasks. What are you wanting or needing to tackle in your life? Perhaps now is the time to add some grit, or determination, to your plans.

H is for Humility

"absence of pride"

Having humility allows us to acknowledge the fact that we are spiritual beings and that we need to be open to our own spiritual needs, as well as those of others. Pride can keep us from showing the goodness of our spirits. It is one thing to take pride in what we do, but when we let pride become bigger than us, we risk starting to believe that ego is more important than our spirit. Once that happens, it is difficult to be receptive to the graces that come with being humble. We cannot not do something just because we might not be appreciated for it. When we do good deeds, expecting only acknowledgement or appreciation, we will be disappointed, let down. We must always be humble enough to extend our helping hand to a fellow spirit. When we help from a kind heart, or place of humility, we won't notice if, or when, we don't receive praise for a good deed.

Humility helps us in understanding that every spiritual being is seeking acceptance, while pride causes us to fear more demands on our time. With pride, it is all about self, what we want, what is in it for me or what is my reward for doing the task. With spirit, we humbly admit that we have needs just like everyone else. By reaching out to others and meeting their needs, we meet our own needs as well. Feeling good by helping someone else and expecting nothing in return, even a thank you, brings our spirit joy and a sense of well-being.

Start today by embracing humility and be rewarded by those who appreciate kindness from kindred spirits. As you go along, you won't notice one way or the other who is gracious and who is not—because you are helping from a humble heart not from ego or self. Let humility, not ego, rule your heart today.

I is for Inspiration

"to affect creativity"

We are not just spiritual beings; we are also creative beings. Whether we are gardeners, bakers, scientists, architects, loan officers or engineers, our minds are always creating—creating a life we can be happy with and, possibly, one in which we can use our creativity to meet our daily living needs. Some of us are more creative than others and can either support ourselves with that passion or use it to do a hobby in our spare time. This creative passion can be art-based, such as oil- or water-painting, stained-glass, pottery, sewing, and candle- or soap-making. It can be musical or mechanical—where we restore old vehicles or help to keep a large manufacturing plant in operation. It can even be an outdoor interest, such as fishing, hunting, or scuba-diving. Can you see yourself doing any of these for fun or work, or having your own craft shop or charter business?

Whatever gift or skill we were blessed with or whichever career or hobby we are "called" to choose, our spirits are happiest when we are creating and sharing our passion with others. What is your inspiration? How do you inspire yourself or others with your creativity? Are you creative only sometimes or all the time? Do you have several creative outlets or only one?

If you already embrace a certain creative passion, what are some ways you can share it more fully with others—family, friends, a social base?

If you are still searching for your special creativity, what is one thing you enjoy doing? Perhaps it can be developed more fully.

When we share our creativity with others, we give them the opportunity to improve theirs, or find that they, too, have a skill to share with others after all.

J is for Joy

"great delight"

Our spirits take great delight in little things—a lone flower, the smell of rain, a cool breeze on a hot day, our favorite song. The more we take joy in the small things, the more we learn to take joy in and appreciate the big things. Our families. Our friends. Our jobs. Our history. Our existence.

To take more delight in or experience greater joy, we must pause to let our spirit appreciate all that we have in our life: not only the air we breathe but the breath we take in and what this means; the sky above us and the ground beneath us and how we are affected by day and night and the changing weather; our family and friends and how good times build community and also how hard times, once worked through, build unity.

There is much for our spirits to be joyful about. Being aware of these things helps us to get through tough times. When our spirits sag under stress, despair, separation, grief or depression, inner joy can help us rise above hard times to a place of peace and contentment, and even bring us to action.

Over the years, I have learned that nothing stays the same. When we are in the throes of joy or sadness, we think the emotion will last forever. The next thing we know our hearts are filled with a different emotion. When we realize and accept that we are ever-changing, our inner joy will be more readily accessible —not just in good times but also in the hard times when it is most needed.

So, the next time you are down, remember, the feeling won't last forever, for joy is right around the corner.

K is for Kindness

"loving nature"

Our spirits are meant to be loving and kind, free of injury or greed. Just as an animal becomes mean when mistreated, so will a human spirit. Care must be taken in every encounter to be kind to the spirit that lives in each of us. It is so easy to be too tired or too busy and not be loving to others. If we are to become more loving spirits, we must practice kindness to every spirit we meet no matter how they act or what they look like—or how we may feel.

Lessons can be taken from our pets. No matter how we might neglect them or accidently step on or kick them, they are still loving toward us and happily greet us every time we return home. I know mine does. She is always underfoot, too, so these things happen. I don't know how many times I think she isn't there, and then one wrong turn and I have stepped on her or nearly tripped over her trying not to step on her. Have you done the same? It is this way with people, too. There are those who love us and want to spend time with us, but we are too busy to see it. So, what happens? They get their feelings hurt. It happens to us, too. We want so much to be a part of someone's life, but it doesn't happen. We grow distant and disheartened by the lack of connection. Kindness calls us to be loving anyway, to understand when someone doesn't have time for us. Kindness also calls us to take time for others, even when it is easier not to try.

When we choose to remain kind despite disappointment, we will be more naturally loving and unaffected by another's behavior. Keep being loving and kind, and your spirit will grow more fully into the you that you are meant to be.

L is for Love

"tender affection"

Every spirit has the capacity for love. From the moment we are born, we are receiving love from our parents and siblings and our extended family and later our friends. Having tender affection for others, even in the face of another's grief, despair, or anger, shows that we honor their spirit and that we care for them. As we appreciate receiving love or tender affection, others appreciate the same—even if they pretend otherwise.

Often, when faced with the negative emotions of others, we don't know how to respond to them. But, if we trust that love and kindness should always be our go-to-place when interacting with others, then we will find the right response, even if it is simply just to listen or to sit in silence with someone as they grieve or try to figure things out. Many times, the loving response is to give space to the person in need to heal and tend to the things they need to get done.

There is a movie quote that says, "Love means never having to say you're sorry." I first heard it when I was quite young. It did not make sense to me then, and it still does not make sense to me today. To me, if you love someone, then it is always important to say you are sorry as soon as you realize you have done something to upset another person. The sooner a hurt is healed the better. And, if it is something still weighing heavily on your heart or spirit, it is never too late to attempt to mend a long ago hurt.

Try not to let fear ever keep you from reaching out to anyone with love in your heart. Your loved one will appreciate it. Wouldn't you in the same place?

M is for Moment

"this instant"

We can be so funny about time. Many of us tend to live in the past, nursing grievances of long ago or romancing a time when life seemed to be happier, less demanding. Some of us live in the future, dreaming of a place that is more successful or less stressful. The happiest spirits are often those who live every instant of their life in the present, being real and being gracious.

Living in the moment is the best place to be, even if it means facing ourselves and adjusting our life, so that we can be happier now...less stressed out now. If we want a different career, house, car, or social network, the best time to make a change is in the moment. Our spirit must, in this instant, decide to get real, set a goal, and make a plan; then, in the next moment, work hard toward that change.

For me, one occasion that required being more in the moment was when I transitioned from living at home into adulthood and my first apartment. A few other occasions were when my husband and I moved from one city to another, several times over the span of a few years. It was difficult to leave the comfort and routine of one home, just when getting settled in, only to start over in an unfamiliar city. Focusing on the moment though made it easier to adjust.

Living in this instant brings clarity. Making the best of each moment helps us to meet the next moment in the best light. What are some occasions that have called you to focus more on living in the moment? Try living today in the present moment, and see how calm your spirit becomes, even when faced with a bad day or unexpected situation. So now, how will you meet your next moment?

N is for Natural

"with ease"

Many people I know, myself included, are filled with stress. Stress from our jobs. Stress from traffic. Stress from our lifestyles. Stress from our boss's expectations or that of our family and friends. Stress from social media. And, stress from society in general including politics and peer pressure. How can we ever feel at ease when we are constantly battling any of these stresses?

Good question. One way is to learn to just let go and let it be. Another way is to find your natural state of being. How does your spirit, or your inner self, like to relax? What can you do to reach that place of stress-free living and be at ease with anything and everything around you? How can you feel easier about what is happening within you or in the wider world beyond you?

I believe it is essential to question our spirit and find our stress triggers. When we learn how to reduce our stressors or lessen their effect on us, we can reach a more natural state of being. Once we do this, it can be our go-to-place when the stresses of this world are zeroing in on us.

Not sure how to start? Why not try some of the other ideas in this book, such as "D is for Dancing," "M is for Moment," or "Y is for Yoga"? In addition, reading books by other authors specializing in stress relief or relaxation can be very helpful. Any time we spend learning how to combat everyday stress, in whatever form it affects us, will be good for our spirit. And being at ease with ourselves is not only good for us, it puts others around us at ease, as well.

What are some ways you can ease any stress in your life and become more relaxed? Think of one way you could start today to be more at ease in your spirit.

O is for Openness

"transparent"

An open spirit is a free spirit, easy to be with, a joy to be around. A transparent spirit can be themselves—free of fear, judgment or melodrama.

One of the things I admire most in another person is their ability to be open, honest, and transparent. They have no fear of being misunderstood. They share their ideas, opinions, beliefs and do not waste time wondering if they will be accepted or doubted. They live honestly and are not afraid to be themselves. There is no malice or falseness about them. That is a spirit I strive to be. Free from lies, deceit, and the fear of being found out that I am not who I let on to be.

When striving to better connect with our own spirit, we should try to own up to something when we are being named as a culprit. If the deed was sound, we should be confident enough to say, "It was me," rather than hiding or taking offense. Even if the outcome isn't what we expected, owning up to mistakes, or things we have said, makes it easier for people to respect us and not only believe us when we need them to, but also question the situation instead of just pointing fingers.

It took me years to learn how to own up to mistakes or poor choices. Being haunted by something I did in the second grade, which I proceeded to deny, finally made me realize it is far better to be honest and face the consequences early on than to wonder what would have happened if I had just "fessed up" right away.

Being honest—taking responsibility, owning our decisions and mistakes, without fear—makes our spirit more loveable, and free of drama. When we try being more open or transparent, the next time we are put on the spot, we might be pleasantly surprised.

P is for Peace

"free from conflict"

The happiest of people are at peace with themselves and the world around them. As spiritual beings, we are most content when we are free from conflict. Of course, it's not easy to stay this way. But, one of our goals should be to strive for a life as free from conflict as possible. Whether we have had a long-standing difference of opinion with a sibling or a misunderstanding with a co-worker, our goal should be, at least, to not create or contribute to more conflict.

Every spirit has a viewpoint, and if we cannot understand that of others, we need to at least respect that they have a right to their own opinion. Then, let it go. Often, just letting a grievance be free of our involvement and be given permission to be what it chooses or needs to be is enough to disperse any hard feelings or anxiety. It is important to take a stand for something, but it is also important to know when taking a stand is the right thing to do and when choosing peace is the better path to take.

As spiritual beings, it is important to be at peace with the world around us. Are you at peace with your world? What things can you let go of that are keeping you from the best version of yourself? Can you picture what your life will be like if you reconcile yourself to others and let yourself be free of conflict? What does being at peace feel like to you?

Take time today to imagine how you can be freer from conflict and more at peace in the world around you. What one step can you take to get you closer to that goal? Is it mending fences with a neighbor? Is it chatting with a dear friend? Is it shutting the news off at an earlier hour than usual? Keep thinking.

Q is for Querist

"inquisitive"

Amazingly, spiritual beings are inquisitive by nature. Even before we begin crawling, our eyes are exploring our surroundings. We are searching to understand where we are, how things work, and how safe our environment is. If we are not questioning where we came from, why we are where we currently are or where we are heading, then we need to consider doing so.

One of the smartest things we can do for our spirit is to question everything—and then, question the answer that we arrived at. By questioning our initial findings, we can be assured that we have arrived at the right answer for ourselves. Being sure of the final answer to our questionings is important. It not only gives us the confidence to respond with a definite yes or no, it also gives us permission to be even more curious about everything around us.

If you are not naturally inquisitive, it may take a bit to get acquainted with questioning one thing much less everything. That is okay. Take your time formulating what it is you have questions to. The more we question, the more we can be open to the idea that what is right for one person may not be what is right for us. Being inquisitive is then a good thing. Questioning helps us when we experience doubt, hesitancy, or false results. Being inquisitive helps us to find the answers to the deepest questions of our heart and mind.

What are your questions? What are you seeking to learn? Start today and seek the answers to your deepest questions. Doing so will lead you closer to your intended purpose and help you to reach that best version of your spiritual self. So, go ahead, be inquisitive.

R is for Realism

"practical"

As spirits grow, we are to practice being realistic. This does not mean we have to live without fun in our lives, but it does mean we should strive for less idealism and more realism. When we are too idealistic, we become unhappy with the way things are, as we focus on what we think our life, or a certain situation, should be. By trying to be realistic, or practical, we can see things more clearly.

It is too easy to let ourselves be fooled by many situations that are not what we think they are. And, we can jump to conclusions too easily when we only know part of the story. It isn't until we learn more about a situation that we realize we needed more information from the start before we could form an objective viewpoint. With time and experience, we learn to question things and observe better before making judgments.

We must always be seeking a full picture—all angles, every viewpoint—in each situation or segment of our life. Being real helps us to be grounded, more balanced. We can then find pleasure in being practical rather than seeking ideals that may not even suit our spirit.

What situations in your life don't make sense to you? What one thing has you wondering if it is real? If you cannot ask anyone about it, put your question into verbal or written form. Ask God or your higher power to help you find what is real. Consider all aspects. Make lists of facts. Research what you can. Discern the possibilities. Meditate on what is true and what is not. Then, let it go. When the real answer or situation presents itself to you, your spirit will know.

S is for Silence

"stillness"

In the silence of one's mind, the spirit often finds the answers the heart is seeking. Without stillness, the busyness of life can drown out our goals, desires, dreams and smother efforts of action and success. The spirit requires an equal amount of excitement or energy and of quiet time to recharge, reflect and reignite the vision of a dream, the glimpse of an idea, the completion of a plan.

When we take time to rest and reflect, we can get in touch with that part of ourselves—our spirit—in a way noise cannot let us. Recently, I was on a deadline to finish a project. I couldn't seem to master the mindset that I needed to focus and get it done. I finally turned off all the sound I could—TV, radio, cell phone, and unnecessary appliances—and set myself to accomplish the task. In just a short time, I was able to complete the project. It felt good. Had I not stilled myself to silence the distractions, I am sure I would not have finished timely.

When is the last time you have paused to consider where your life is heading and if you need more silence to get where you want or need to be? Are you happy with the path you are choosing? Is there something about your life you would like to change? Is your spirit happy with the person you present to others or the part of yourself that you hide from them? What are some areas that need improvement? Do you need more stillness in your life to contemplate these changes and learn which direction to take or decision to make?

Take time now for silence. Yes, you may still hear the birds sing or the traffic rush, but quiet your mind and let your spirit be free of the noise in your life. What do you hear speaking to you from the center of your being?

T is for Trust

"confident expectation"

As spiritual beings, we need trust in our life and relationships. One of the best gifts we can give another is our trust. But what exactly is trust? It is the confident expectation that our loved one or acquaintance will not let us down. They will meet us as planned. They will keep a confidence. They will not cheat us or steal from us. They will not lie about us. Once a trust is broken, it is difficult to gain that trust back. When a trust has been broken, spirit must pull on all its other reserves or gifts such as forgiveness, grace, communication and the desire to be at peace with everyone—most especially, the one who has let us down.

And then, there is the question if we are being trustworthy for others. Is our spirit granting trust in others automatically? Or, are we hesitant, waiting to see if the other is trustworthy or not?

When I was in grade school, I befriended the new girl in class. No one seemed to be asking her to be their friend, so I decided to reach out to her. We spent our recess and lunch talking and sharing. I was out sick for a day, and when I returned, I discovered all I had told her was classroom news. I learned several valuable lessons from it. Most important was not letting the experience keep me from trusting again. The next person I trusted is now my best friend to this day.

Sure, it can be a personal risk, but confidently expecting someone else to keep our trust is far better than withholding it. By being trustworthy and giving our trust to others first, we build community and we honor our spirit and theirs.

Give your confident expectation of trust to someone today and discover new possibilities in your ever-evolving relationships—with others and your own spirit.

U is for Understanding

"sympathetic awareness"

To understand one another is one of the greatest gifts we can give to someone. We may not always agree with our fellow spirit travelers on this planet, but we can certainly strive to give them sympathy in times of sadness, grief, despair, depression or any of the many other human emotions that we all experience in varying degrees. When we develop an understanding of our own self, we can embrace our spirit more fully and be better able to be there for others.

By being aware of how we or our loved one, friend, co-worker or neighbor is feeling, we can be more sympathetic. Whether we offer words of comfort or wisdom, give hugs or our shoulder to lean on, or simply listen quietly and sympathetically, we are providing an understanding environment with space for that spirit to be oneself, to let go, to share, and to heal. If some awkwardness occurs, remember, we are all on the same journey to be the best versions of our spiritual selves. So, why not embrace that awkwardness as a sign that spirit is growing past its own comfort zone?

Reaching out to others in sympathetic awareness is the beginning of the best relationship we can have with our own spirit. The next time you are presented with the opportunity to be sympathetic, take time to listen. For it is in listening to our fellow spirits that we gain understanding. When we understand better, we can be more kind, more loving, more compassionate toward them. And, becoming more aware of what is really happening can lead our spirit to be more sympathetic to others just when they need us the most.

V is for Vigilance

"watchful"

If we are in tune with our spirit, we can say that we are being watchful not to fall into a life of mediocrity, a life where we act like we don't know who we are or where we are going. We must always be vigilant to stay alert to our self—our core being, what we like and don't like, what we believe in or stand for, where we hope to be in 20 or 30 years. By being watchful, we can be aware of when it is time to change jobs, when we need to reach out to a friend, take a certain online course or join a particular club. And when we are alert, we can more easily know when we need to, simply, step back and slow down.

Having spiritual vigilance is like having a compass. It gives us the ability to see where we are going and when we need fine-tuning, whether it be added inspiration, more quiet time, or less busyness. Try being vigilant today. Where is your compass pointing?

Ask yourself where you are heading? Will this direction get you to the goal you set for yourself yesterday? If you are heading in the right direction for the major parts of your life, are you happy in the other smaller areas of your life? Are you happy with you? If so, that is great; but if not, take some time today to ask yourself, "How can I be more careful to stay on the path I have set for myself?" or, "What can I do to get on a better suited path for my future?" Then, make one minor adjustment in the right direction, so tomorrow you can be on a truer course for yourself. Trust me, five or ten years from now, your spirit will thank you for taking time—now—for being aware of the life decisions, big and small, you are making along the way.

W is for Willingness

"at the ready"

As spiritually aware beings, we must always have a willingness to be that person who knows when flexibility is needed in ourselves or when a kindness needs to be extended to another. Being at the ready challenges us to step forward out of our comfort zone to a place of hospitality, a place where we are not inconvenienced by the surprises of life but ready to handle them with grace, humor, and kindness. We may not or cannot always be prepared for some things, but we can develop the willingness to help in the face of despair, to listen when someone needs to talk, and to pitch in when no one else can be available.

Our mind often prevents spirit from helping, as it fills with all kinds of fear of the unknown. The load might be too heavy, cost too much, or take me too far out of my way. Often though, it is less of an inconvenience than first anticipated. That errand was done on our way home, and helping our neighbor gave us the chance to learn something new. It is the dread, or fear, of being bothered or inconvenienced that can keep us from saying yes to a request.

Since I have become aware of how fear keeps people from offering help to others, I am less resistant to extending my helping hand. Now, I am more ready than ever to assist another when asked to help. And, when a request has been more than I can achieve, I instead offer the person other options to help out.

Let's not let our mind, or fearful thoughts, keep us from helping a fellow spirit on life's road have a better day. Being at the ready can bring our spirits peace, joy and serenity. So, ask yourself today how you can be more willing to help when asked. Why not let your spirit be ready and willing for your next adventure?

23

X is for Xeriscape

"requiring little maintenance"

Although xeriscaping is in reference to maintaining our yards and to providing an environment of least care for our lawn or landscape, we can take a lesson and learn what we need to do to provide our spirit with the right amount of self-care. Just as our bodies need food and exercise, our spirits need reflection and recreation. By learning how much time we may need for quiet time or meditation, further education, inspiration, rest, fun, relaxation or rejuvenation, we will eventually know the signals of our spirit that tell us when it's time to step back and rest or take a class to enhance certain skills or have a friend date.

Spiritual xeriscaping is all about learning who we are and listening to the cues of our soul. By doing so, we can stay spiritually hydrated. There will be no drought—or "burnout." We will be well-maintained and not find ourselves in a place of desperation.

What can you do to help your spirit be more well-tuned and require less maintenance in busy times? Take time today to learn what works for you. Is it music? Could it be reading? Or maybe even a nap? How about dancing? The investment is little, but the reward is much.

Devoting time to "hydrating" your spirit can bring you to the much-needed centeredness you've been searching for. Slow down today and do one thing to nurture your spirit, so that tomorrow you can better handle any stress you may face. You won't be disappointed by investing some personal maintenance now. Try it. Spiritually xeriscape today—rest, listen to favorite soothing sounds, read or even nap—and be pleasantly pleased with the results of your self-maintenance.

Y is for Yoga

"freedom from self"

To be spiritually free, we must be free from self, or more specifically, free of ego. Ego is that part of us which seeks recognition for all that we do or all that we accomplish. Our ego chooses things over others. Ego wants to rule. Slowly, spirit gets smothered, and we lose sight of all that is important and most especially ourselves.

Ego is great when we need the energy to achieve a goal or launch a plan. But for spirit to breathe, we must keep ego in his or her place. Once done, spirit is better able to accept any accolades with grace and humility.

When we are free from self (ego), spirit can choose what is next for our journey or path because spirit knows—or should know—our true self, the self that counts. When our ego allows our spirit to truly know what we like, love, and enjoy doing, or feels called to do, we can be free to be at our best.

When we do yoga, we may be stretching our physical selves, but—spiritually—yoga is helping us to separate that which is ego-based from that which benefits what is best for our spirit. Yoga, therefore, can help us to become more centered and connected to ourselves—physically and spiritually.

Yoga is not for everyone, but the same results can be found through meditation; other methods of stretching, strengthening, and toning the body; long, peaceful walks; and even naps. When is the last time you took a break from self? Take some time today to consider ways that will help you to become more spiritually centered or balanced. Then, choose a way that brings the connection you are seeking, at this moment, into your life.

Z is for Zeal

"excitement"

As spiritual beings, we should be experiencing more zeal or excitement in our lives. More happiness. More joy. More gratefulness. More appreciation for all that we have today. A place to live. A job. Abilities to do and accomplish our goals. The love of family and friends. But...we get caught up in our lack of more time, a better job, more pay, dependable friends and so on. Focusing on what we lack will negatively affect the positive aspects that bring our spirits excitement.

Zeal is good for us. When we focus on all that is good in our life, our spirits can soar. We get excited about our future and start to take action to bring about more good things to our way of living. This zeal can carry us forward in ways being indifferent cannot. Zeal motivates us to be excited about accomplishing all sorts of things from finishing a project, getting chores done, or calling a long lost but once dear friend. Not being excited about life, or certain tasks or goals, keeps us from getting anything done.

The next time you feel unmotivated—question the source. Do you feel sad? Are you fearful? Once you identify the reason for your inertia, you can work toward finding an answer. By appreciating what you have, focusing on the bright side of life and motivating yourself, your outlook will improve. You will be more cheerful and get more things done. Being more excited and feeling less down will bring more positive results for you. Eventually, zeal will reveal itself with more smiles, a skip in your step, even a whistle to a favorite tune. Soon, you'll be asked, "What's up?" "Why the happy face?" All because your spirit is full of joy.

Zeal is contagious. So, be sure to share it with a fellow spirit.

Afterthoughts

So, there you have it. Twenty-six ways to embrace your spirit.

It is my hope and prayer that at least one idea in this book has inspired you to embrace your spirit more fully. May it help you not only become a better you, but also become more fully connected to all that is you. May you, especially, have a clearer understanding of yourself as a spiritual being. And, may what you've read bring you closer to whatever "more" it is that you are seeking for your spirit, whether it is being more kind, more joyful, more at peace, or more in the moment.

If you were inspired yet want more of what you have read in this book, please look for future works. Some may be different than this one, but there will be similar ones, even a "Honor One Another (Book II)." I say this because there was so much more that I wanted to share with you in this book.

For each letter, I chose one topic word. However, I so easily could have chosen a different one and, in fact, wanted to include more than one topic on several of the letters. For the letter C, I considered Courage. For the letter F, I wanted to give Forgiveness an Honorary Mention. For the letter G, I went with Grit, as it spoke more to me at this writing, and yet I still wanted to spotlight Grace. And, for the letter M, I wanted to share Mantra, Meditation and Magnificence with you; although, as you have read, Moment finally won out. If you go back to the Introduction of this book, you will find included there, K is for Kaleidoscope and N is for Namaste. These two topics enhanced what I wanted to share with you in my introductory thoughts and also allowed me the opportunity to include in the body of this book, K is for Kindness and N is for Natural...a bonus that I hope you enjoyed and will benefit from.

Still, there were more of these second and third topics that I wanted to share with you. But this could so easily make for—as one of my college professors once wrote down the side margin of one of my essay assignments in reference to my lengthy sentence structure—a "long and winding" book. In this case, I wanted you, my reader, to be inspired, not overwhelmed. So, one topic per page was my end goal. I have learned that all we need is a small amount of encouragement, or inspiration, to get and keep us going...for a long time to come.

Before I close, please remember that with every encounter, we are always changing, growing, evolving. Not just ourselves but everyone. Our spirits seek transformation, even when we don't realize it. A case in point is with my dad when I was in high school. He was tending his rose garden, which took up about a fifth of the property we lived on. Late one morning I went out to remind him that it was almost time to take me to school. As he trimmed and snipped here and there, and watered, I asked him why he had planted so many roses. There were so many colors and varieties—red, purple, pink, yellow, orange, white, mixed... hybrids, climbing, miniature and so on. Each rose bush even had its own name. He said, "I plant them for your mom. I know she loves roses; they're her favorite flower. I've been hoping they'll make her happy." That conversation stayed with me. My dad was a quiet man and those were the most words he had ever spoken to me at one time. As years went by, I came to realize it was his way of trying to show my mom that he had changed, that he wasn't the same man he was in their early years together. And I knew that if my dad's spirit could transform for the better that everyone's spirit can too, as they journey down life's road.

In your search for your identity, purpose, or higher calling, please know that everyone goes through this search. It is normal for us to question all sorts of things —if we have a spirit or not, what our purpose is, and if we are on the right path in our life. Just like I have, you too will find your purpose and learn ways to embrace your spirit more fully. Keep on doing what you are doing. Keep on questioning. Keep on searching and researching. Keep on living, laughing, loving, giving and doing all those things that make you so uniquely you. Keep reading and learning. Keep making friends. Keep working. If you are not happy with your job, consider other possibilities—either by developing better skills or by taking classes in the field which you are really interested in. If you don't have a hobby but want a distraction from your day job, reflect on what you would enjoy doing or what would be rewarding for you to share with others. If you want to give back to society for all that you have, check out volunteer opportunities within a five-mile radius of your home. Whatever you choose to do, whether it is to take up a new fitness interest, a book or movie club, devote time for prayer or meditation—or even write a book, it will lead you to embrace your spirit more fully and eventually to find your purpose.

Reflection is important. Action is important. The journey is important.

So, don't give up. Things take time. Whatever your search is, whether it is to become more spiritual, to be inspired to new heights or to become more of the you that you are meant to be, I know you will find it.

Always and ever,

Virg

References

Definitive phrases are from Webster's New World Dictionary of the American Language, Second College Edition; 1979.

"B is for Beatitude" is referenced from <u>Matthew 5:3–10</u>, New American Bible, Oxford University Press; Oxford, New York; 1995.

Quote: *"Love is never having to say you're sorry"* from the movie, Love Story (1970), starring Ryan O'Neal and Ali MacGraw.

Further Reading

Virg has read many books that have influenced her life and writing. These are a few of her favorites:

"Take Time" by Vera Holding; 1966; Quality Printing Co., Inc.

"Luvly You! Loveable You!" by Char Crawford (no relation); 1973; Zondervan Publishing House.

"Loving Yourself for God's Sake" by Adolfo Quezada; 1997; Resurrection Press, Ltd.

Enjoy!

About the Author

Virginia Alice Crawford has been a writer ever since she learned to write in the first grade. Part of her writing journey includes keeping a diary; writing letters to family and friends; writing essays, poems, short stories and even an epitaph; producing family and community newsletters; being a church bulletin editor for 17 plus years; and teaching journaling classes to young writers. Virg, as she prefers, lives in Texas with her husband of 32 years and her devoted long-haired, mini Dachshund, Sammie Jolene. She is the proud "mah" of her son and her daughter-in-law—both teachers—and proud "mee-mah" and "grammy" of two precious "grandbabes." In addition to writing, Virg enjoys sewing small non-clothing projects, photo-scrapbooking, and hiking in the great outdoors. Virg's goal in life is to inspire others to achieve their dreams; love more and be kind; always believe the best before thinking the worst; never give up; always have faith that one's spirit will be led to where it needs to be; and never ever let fear hold you back, instead use it as a stepping stone to the next chapter of your life.

Contact Information

To contact Virg, you can email or send a letter to her at:

honeysucklepublishingllc@yahoo.com

Virginia Alice Crawford
Honeysuckle Publishing, LLC
PO Box 1163
Three Rivers, TX 78071

www.ingramcontent.com/pod-product-compliance
Lightning Source LLC
Chambersburg PA
CBHW031541040426

42445CB00010B/649